THAT'S SO FUNNY I FELL OFF MY DINOSAUR LAUGHING!

Michael J. Pellowski

A TRUMPET CLUB ORIGINAL BOOK

Published by
The Trumpet Club
666 Fifth Avenue
New York, New York 10103

ISBN: 0-440-84015-5

Printed in the United States of America

September 1988

10 9 8 7 6 5 4 3 2

KRI

Why are dinosaurs extinct?
Maybe they all died laughing!
Read these jokes
and judge for yourself!

HOLD ON TIGHT!

When does a dinosaur wake up?

At the dawn of time.

Why are dinosaurs never late?

Because they are early lizards.

Why was it easy to go to school in prehistoric times?

Because there was no history to study.

What did the dinosaur say to the caveman who insulted him?

"Sticks and stones may break my bones but names will never hurt me."

What did the triceratops do when he saw another dinosaur in his path?

He honked one of his three horns.

What has three horns, eight wheels and weighs 60,000 lbs.?

A triceratops on roller skates.

Why should you never ask a brontosaurus to tell a bedtime story?

Because their tails are very long.

Which dinosaur is very dull?

A Bronto-Bore-Us.

How did the brontosaurus come to weigh 80,000 lbs.?

He ate too many desserts.

Why do they call a brontosaurus a thunder lizard?

If you heard a hungry brontosaurus's stomach rumble, you'd know why.

What kind of dishes do stegosauruses eat off of?

Armor plates.

What does a tyrannosaurus on a diet have for lunch?

A brontosaurus and a diet soda.

Why is lava like a stolen diamond?

They're both hot rocks.

Do dinosaurs age gracefully?

No, they end up looking like old fossils.

What do you get when a brontosaurus sits on a zero?

Nothing flat.

What is a tyrannosaurus's favorite dessert?

Brontosaurus a la mode.

Why are brontosauruses so spacey?

Because their heads are always in the clouds.

Why did Mama brontosaurus name her baby *Drizzle?*

Because he was just a little thunder beast.

SAY
WHAT?
RIDDLES

What did the glacier say to Mother Earth?

"Freeze! I've got you covered!"

What did the caveman say when his spear broke in two?

"Now I'll have to join the club."

What did the brontosaurus say after he got a spanking?

"Dino-sore."

What did the tyrannosaurus say when he saw a prehistoric horse?

"Ah, fast food for lunch!"

What did one volcano say to the other?

"Don't smoke. It's bad for your health."

What does a mammoth use to wash its tusks?

Ivory soap.

PREHISTORIC PUZZLES?

What do you get when you cross a chicken and a duck-billed dinosaur?

A cluck-billed dinosaur.

What do you get when you cross a brontosaurus fossil and chicken broth?

The world's biggest soup bone.

What do you get when you cross a flock of sheep and an Ice Age elephant?

A very woolly mammoth.

What do you get when you cross a dentist and a tyrannosaurus?

A dinosaur that spends all of its time flossing its teeth.

What do you get when you cross a sword and a prehistoric cat?

A saber-toothed tiger.

What do you get when you cross a skunk and a brontosaurus?

The biggest stinker in the world!

What do you get if you cross a tyrannosaurus and a dog?

A pet that needs a very strong muzzle.

What do you get when you cross a pterodactyl and a savings account?

The biggest nest egg in history.

What do you get if you cross a dinosaur egg and a herd of cows?

Eggnog for a thousand.

What do you get if you cross a brontosaurus and a gopher?

Something that digs holes bigger than the Grand Canyon.

What do you get if you cross a dinosaur and a cactus?

The world's biggest porcupine.

What do you get if you cross a frog and a tyrannosaurus?

A dinosaur that catches pterodactyls on its tongue and eats them.

What do you get if you cross a rooster and a brontosaurus?

I don't know, but when it crows, *everyone* wakes up.

What do you get if you cross a brontosaurus and a football player?

A quarterback *no one* can tackle.

NOW
WE'RE
MOVING!

How does a six-ton brontosaurus sit on its dinosaur eggs?

Very carefully.

What does a tyrannosaurus eat at a barbecue?

Brontoburgers and potato salad.

How do you make breakfast for two thousand cavemen?

Fry up exactly *one* dinosaur egg.

Who was the world's first health food nut?

The brontosaurus. He was strictly a vegetarian.

What do duck-billed dinosaurs cook their food in?

Quack pots.

What weighs six tons, wears a mask and says "trick or treat?"

A brontosaurus on Halloween.

YOU'D BETTER HANG ON NOW!

Who is the silliest dinosaur?

The daffy duck-billed dinosaur.

Why would stegasauruses make good football players?

They already have spikes.

What's gigantic and bumps into mountains?

A brontosaurus playing blind man's bluff.

Which dinosaur is very noisy at night?

The Tyrannosnore.

Who is the dumbest dinosaur?

The duck-billed dinosaur. He's a birdbrain.

What's worse than a saber-toothed tiger with a toothache?

A brontosaurus with a sore neck.

PREHISTORIC PARALLELS!

"I'm going to bite you, dinosaur," the tyrannosaurus snapped.

"I hate being so woolly," said the mammoth sheepishly.

"I hit him with my club," said the caveman bluntly.

"I'm mad enough to erupt," said the volcano hotly.

"I ate sour fruit," said the caveman bitterly.

"I don't like the Ice Age," said the dinosaur coolly.

"I can break dinosaur eggs," the caveman cracked.

"We can't put these fossil bones together," said the scientist puzzledly.

"You can't chew through my armor plates," said the stegosaurus toughly.

"I can fly!" said the pterodactyl loftily.

"I have two brains," said the brontosaurus very thoughtfully.

CAVEMAN CHUCKLES!

What did the hippy caveman say to his tailor?

"Hey, buddy, give me some skin."

What did the caveman say to the scientist?

"Don't try to make a monkey out of me."

Why are cavemen like rich ladies?

They both wear fur coats when they go out.

What did the hobo caveman say when he saw the cave tribe eating dinner?

"Can you spear me a piece of meat?"

What kind of music do cavemen like?

Rock music.

What did the caveman have for lunch?

A club sandwich.

What does a caveman do when he gets mad?

He goes ape.

What does a caveman need to fix a broken weapon?

Spear parts.

What do cavemen like to drink?

Club soda.

What do you call four cavemen trying to play music on boulders?

A rock band.

What is the favorite sport of cavemen?

Golf, because they get to use clubs.

What did the caveman do when he saw a thunder lizard?

He ran lightning fast.

DINOSAUR DAZZLERS!

What part of a cave is the noisiest?

The mouth of the cave.

Why did the tyrannosaurus have a million-dollar dentist bill?

He had all of his teeth capped.

What is the hardest part about driving a dinosaur?

Finding a parking place big enough.

What do you get when a brontosaurus applauds?

A clap of thunder beast.

What do you get if you cross a witch and the Ice Age?

A very long cold spell.

What lives in prehistoric times and flies?

A brontosaurus on a hang glider.

How did you go fishing in prehistoric times?

First you baited a hook with an 8,000-lb. worm.

What did the tyrannosaurus say when he saw a mammoth in a block of ice?

"Oh boy, a frozen dinner!"

What does a tyrannosaurus want for Easter?

A chocolate brontosaurus.

Why is it hard for saber-toothed tigers to go on a diet?

Because they are *mammoth* eaters.

Why should you never take an iguanodon to a factory?

Because iguanodons are plant eaters.

What was the hardest part of preparing a Thanksgiving meal in prehistoric times?

Stuffing the brontosaurus.

PREHISTORIC PERPLEXES?

The fossil of an early horse?

. . . a bony pony.

A dinosaur that can work magic?

. . . a lizard wizard.

A curse on a meat-eating dinosaur?

. . . a tyrannosaurus rex hex.

The Lone Ranger's dinosaur?

. . . Bronto Tonto.

A mammoth that picks on smaller animals?

. . . a woolly bully.

A fad during the Ice Age?

. . . an Ice Age rage.

A group of singing dinosaurs?

. . . a brontosaurus chorus.

A giant bone of a dinosaur?

. . . a colossal fossil.

TYRANNOSAURUS TICKLERS!

What is a tyrannosaurus's favorite sandwich?

Brontosaurus on rye.

What did one tyrannosaurus say to the other?

"I've got a bone to pick with you."

What kind of vitamins do tyrannosauruses take?

Chewable vitamins.

What does a hungry tyrannosaurus say after he meets a new dinosaur?

Burp!

What is tyrannosaurus rex's favorite movie?

JAWS!

What goes *GRRR! GRRR! WHOA! KA-BOOM!?*

A tyrannosaurus slipping on a banana peel.

Why is a tyrannosaurus like a giant cave?

Because they both have big mouths.

How does a tyrannosaurus like his brontosaurus steak?

Raw.

What time is it when a tyrannosaurus sees a brontosaurus?

Dinnertime!

Why is a rubber band like a tyrannosaurus's mouth?

Because they both snap, and when they do, it hurts!

Why is a tyrannosaurus like Paul Bunyon?

They both have big choppers.

What has two wheels and is extremely dangerous?

A tyrannosaurus on a bicycle.

What kind of books do tyrannosauruses like?

They like books they can sink their teeth into.

What do you call a triceratops standing on its head?

A triceratopsy-turvy.

"YOU TELL 'EMS!"

You tell 'em, vol-
cano, you're hot
stuff.

You tell 'em,
cave, you've got
a big mouth.

You tell 'em,
palm tree,
I'll give you a
hand.

You tell 'em,
caveman,
It's your club.

You tell 'em,
dinosaur,
Your memory
goes way back.

You tell 'em,
tyrannosaurus,
and don't speak
with your mouth
full.

You tell 'em, Ice Age, the story chills me to the bone.

You tell 'em, woolly mammoth, I'll shear the blame.

You tell 'em, brontosaurus, start way back at the beginning.

You tell 'em, caveman, they axed for you.

You tell 'em, flying dinosaur, just wing it.

You tell 'em, glacier, I'll just freeze.

You tell 'em, tyrannosaurus, and be sure to tell the tooth.

You tell 'em, saber-toothed tiger, and don't pussyfoot around.

CATCH THAT DINOSAAAUR...!

Why is a tyrannosaurus like a person who likes to gossip?

They both can't keep their mouths shut.

Why was the dinosaur always prompt?

Because he arrived before time began.

What did the duck-billed dinosaur do when the Ice Age came?

He flew south for the era.

What newspaper do pterodactyls deliver?

The *Prehistoric Times*.

What's grey and has a million red spots?

A brontosaurus with the measles.

How do dinosaurs decorate their bathrooms?

With rep-tiles.

What is the favorite meal of cavemen?

Barbecued spear ribs.

What do you get when a brontosaurus plays jump rope?

A severe earthquake.

What's the biggest problem with having a brontosaurus for a watchdog?

Building a doghouse big enough for him.

What kind of dinosaur can fly?

A brontosaurus with a pilot's license.

How can you tell if a volcano is mad?

It will blow its top.

Which dinosaurs are the funniest dinosaurs?

Duck-billed dinosaurs. They're always quacking jokes.

Why don't tyrannosauruses swim?

They can't find bathing trunks big enough to fit them.

What did the cavemen say when he wanted his dog Rex to attack a dinosaur?

He said, "Tyrannosaurus, Rex!"

What wears lipstick and has 10,000 sharp teeth?

A lady tyrannosaurus.

What bounces, rumbles and weighs six tons?

A thunder lizard on a pogo stick.

What do you get when you cross a dinosaur and a wizard?

A Brontosorcerer!

What weighs six tons and goes "Goo-Goo"?

A baby brontosaurus.

How does a mother brontosaurus sit on her eggs?

Very, very carefully.